The Days Of Living & Loving

Zainab Amjad

ISBN 978-93-5610-481-5

Published in India 2022 by Pencil

Contributors:
Illustrator: Vittal Acharya Vandavasu
Editor: Vittal Acharya Vandavasu

A brand of
One Point Six Technologies Pvt. Ltd.
123, Building J2, Shram Seva Premises,
Wadala Truck Terminal, Wadala (E)
Mumbai 400037, Maharashtra, INDIA
E connect@thepencilapp.com
W www.thepencilapp.com

Author biography

Zainab Amjad/Khawaja is a Pakistani poetess who was writing for sometime on Poemhunter.com but later became unknown and silent. Vittal Vandavasu came cross her work on poemhunter, while she was also an ardent reader and critic of Vittal's poetry. This anthology of poems is compiled by Vittal to make a monumental moment of Zainab's works. She is nowhere to be found online and cannot be communicated with anymore. Maybe through this compilation of her poetry, she could be touched in silence.

CONTENTS

A Bit Of Love Everyone Needs

My eyes are blinded,
By things only i can see,
They are deep inside me,
I deal with them each day,

Too many secrets in my heart,
That are eating me slowly,

I wish to be known,
By another,
I wish to be cared,
By the one i love,

Asked for too much,
For all of which,
God gives nothing,

These things i carry inside me,
Will turn to dust,
On your touch,
Just try to love me.

My World Is Dying.

Dark, its so dark,
Quiet, its so quiet,

Love, its weary,
Life, its dreary,

God, he's going,
My soul, it's shaking,

You, are far,
Leaving just a scar,

You were special,
You lived in my heart,

The music has stopped,
The night has passed,

The clock keeps ticking,
My mind just weeps,

I live with a pain...
I live with my soul...

My world is dying,
Love is my crime.

In The Deep Silence...

Even then, when the darkness had fallen,
Resting upon the skies,
Spreading deep silence down there...that seeped,
Across everything,
Quietly and yet so loudly,
Was every heart-aching...

The grey clouds so heavy,
Hovered upon each soul,
Forming a wall of uncertainty,
That night, that stretchingly long night,
Dead was each heart in the face of misery,
Achingly hurtful was the blow each wind threw,
And despite the pain, the acute pain,
That grew in each restless soul,
Nobody in that land of pain knew,
What another soul went through,
Tears fell from those sad eyes,
Whose tragedy none could understand,
And though all were in pain,
Knowing so clearly yet no one knew,
What another soul went through...

Bleeding hearts and hopeless ones still breathed,
Hoping of hope that they didn't see,

Blood from fresh and past wounds was there,
Pooling around so freely,
Guns, blades and knives,
Were powerless this night,
For only God knew,
That such pain in the heart and mind,
Was more painful than torturous death combined,
Served was this in each platter,
By God, the Divine,

Cried so many this night,
Hurt so many this night,
For love,
For loss,
For pain,
For shame,

And this was the game of God,
Which even then, only He knew.

This Love Hurts

I know nothing of your cries,
I know only of my tries,
To tell you That you're not alone,
That I am still by your side
Remain in my heart the feelings I had for you,
-that are true as God is in our lives,

But what, and if you never love me this way,
Like every other heartless one who came,
Will I still smile and laugh that way?
When I believed there was hope to find space in your life,
What, when all hope comes crashing down,
Leaving my heart all empty and used,
The pain ill feel will rest with me,
For lonely nights and days to come, I fear,
Tears upon tears will pool around me,
And what if I never swim through..?

I hear your cries even in the quiet,
But only if my words could soothe you,
Because a time has come when i don't matter,
For all I know, I never mattered,
This time has come when you've gone so far,
Making me feel like I've lost you,
I care so much that it hurts,

To know that you don't want me,
And still, your cries reach me,
But only if these words...this love could also reach you

The Want

There is no point in loving someone so much,
You can hope to get some love back,
And keep hoping until all hope dies,
But the hopes you have can never die,

Wishes you have remain wishes in your heart,
Which no tears, no God can touch,
You can try and try to pretend You're okay,
But all you know is that you're not okay,

A prayer is what then comes from inside,
With tears and tears running down fast,
All you want is for god to help,
Only to find out that answer he won't your prayers,
For sins, you committed in your past,

All might happen for the good,
But what you want can never be for the good,
Why does it matter if you have been wronged,
You can't help it, can stop the want,

For as long as its been you've waited for someone to come,
But came so many just not the one,
You're dying to have him by your side,
But you get to know that he doesn't want your side,

Hate you do your destiny,
Shaped things so cruelly,
Why can't things be the way we want?
Can your love for God make him listen to your heart?

Can he then change what's coming and what's not?
Dreams I dreamt I want to dream again,
And hope that everything will change,
That together we can be someday,

And my God will create some space in that heart,
Which has loved someone else for so long!
I try to stop myself each day,
From having so much conviction in God and love,

For someday everything might break,
And I might have nothing to hold onto,
And the love I sought, I won't ever get,
And tears inside will finally fall down,

But for now, this is all I can wish upon,
I don't want to know that he'll never come,
And if it has to be that way,
I wanna speak to God someday.

Why Is There An End

Where is that eye?
Which was to watch over me tonight...
Where is that heart?
Which was supposed to love me tonight...

I wonder and wonder still,
Why you left me this way,
To broken shadows of happiness now walking away,
To memories of empty dreams now ashes to sway,

Why was this the end?
Why was there an end?
When I ask myself I hear my mind,
Screaming and tearing away,

You did this to me,
For all the reasons you never gave,
What tonight i dont seem to understand,
Is why you even loved me in the first place?

To leave this heart hollow?
To give this soul pain?
Im trembling under this blanket,
Of cold loneliness that remains,

The skies never turn blue,
Time never moves,
What am i to do,
If i keep loving you?

A part of me has gone with you,
To a place where all things disappear,
From where nothing comes back to you,
Even for all your tears,

I look around me,
And find what i dont see,
Your arms that welcomed me,
Are tonight not there,
I whisper a word to myself,
To hear your voice back,
But what comes back is just cold air

I dont have the strength to remain,
What you left of me,
Im weak inside, im falling slowly,
Come back to me,
I miss you so much dear.

The Pain In Me

Tonight, the darkness is kissing my pain,
Holding me loosely,
Cradling my shame,
Soothing an ache stagnated in my heart,
Going it seems but still it does not,
Some blood will drop from my arm,
Hurt it will but a smile it will cause,
For the pain i got,
For the love i gave,
I will smile and smile away my pain,
Smiling i will let myself free,
Let go of the clutches not letting me breathe,
A tear that falls keeps falling it seems,
Dissolving into the dark,
Its darkening it seems,
My presence i dont feel,
My heart so heavy,
Is not making me breathe,
Tonight i just bleed,

Black is what i see in the horizon,
Black is all that is around me,
I am just fitting perfectly,
In the darkness, the deadness around me,
Its easy to let it enter my soul,

To penetrate my heart, my mind, my soul,
Because dead i am,
And dead i remain,
So i shall let the deadness become me.

Forgetting You

The space once there in my heart,
Is now pierced by holes, loving you has caused,
Day and night just thinking of you,
I never knew that this would come too,
I don't know whats happening here today,
All seems lost, I have little left to say,
The distance so long made me ache,
But i told myself that I'd forget you someday,

It was hard, so hard, to grow out of love,
I dont know if I have gotten out as yet,
Once upon a time I smiled at your thought,
Now my heart drenches in pain when memories hit me back,
I hoped for long to see you come my way,
You were almost there, fate turned you away,
I see why god does it, his reasons seem clear,
But the void inside so deep,
Will always remain there,

Belief in happiness seems to be dying away,
But it will all be okay someday,
I wish that life hadn't turned out this way,
But its okay I guess,
It will be okay someday...

What Happened Today...

Im sitting in my classroom today,
My friends are laughing,
But the sound of their laughter never reaches my ear,
I try hard to pull myself out from the lone corner in my own thoughts,
But the harder i struggle the deeper i tread,

The erratic painful beat of my heart,
Gets louder as i feel i cant breathe at all,
I hold back all my tears so no one can see,
What is crushing me, going on inside me,
I rest my head against the wall,
And think of times of my fall,
I try hard, just not to cry,
As the teacher goes on with a lecture it seems to me,

Should i say it directly? a voice says,
Something just happened to me,
It could be we...
My tear falls,
The voice says, but love i wont be able to,
Could it still be we?
My heart flinches,
You still feel the same way?
This is for us..

And then just suddenly the voice leaves me,

Across a wall, that voice i guess speaks to another being,
The voice, which is just now alien to me,
I loved that perfect everything to me,
And now the space between us kills me,
Nothing can fill that space there,
Nothing can fill a heart thats empty,

My love was dealt with so unfairly,
I miss her, her voice, everything,
The way she smelt, the way she laughed,
The way she always made me feel,
I look back and its all hurt and pain,
I can never get over her angelic face,

I try now to stay away from her,
I dont want my feelings to show on my face,
It happened,
Its over. I remember, she said,
She doesnt want another one,

Hope she knew the intensity of my love,
But I had to give in just for the sake of my love,

My mind weeps at all the memories of a sad past,
My heart hurts when for her it still feels the untended love inside,
It never goes, it always stays inside,
Tears fall, I feel them on my arm,
The cuts i see, I hide them quickly,

I bend down pretending to pick my pencil that fell,
I wipe my tears, coming back to the classroom I left...

I Saw It Happen To You

The night is achingly slow,
The violent wind rattles the doors and windows,
All eyes shut,
All minds at sleep,
The disturbance of the night,
Keeps me out of sleep,

I look into the space above and around me,
Trying to search for something in it that remains hidden to me,
It irks me, what I cannot see,
In the silence of the soul I find no serenity,
In restlessness I ask for answers,
Of why it happens,
What happens to you and me,
The night remains silent,
And clueless I remain for what seems like eternity,

The confusion in my mind,
The questions from my pain,
Of why it happens,
What to happens to you and me,
The night remains silent,
And clueless i remain for what seems like eternity,

The confusion in my mind,
The questions from my pain,
Ask me again and again,
Why it happens to you and me,

The memories of hoping for joy,
And the memories of hoping breaking me,
The thoughts of calming myself,
And the calm now killing me,
The thought of those eyes,
Which brought me so close,
The thought of fate,
Which took me so far,
I see where life brings me,

From the corner of this eye,
Holding back its emotions,
I see someone where I had imagined myself to be,
I see a smile which fits on that face so perfectly,
And smiling for that smile and hurting for none on me,
I walk by unnoticed,
Saying a prayer in my aching heart,
To have that smile always on that face,
In myself I laugh at myself for my love's stupidity,
Where everyone's happy theres no happiness in me,
But I walk by quietly knowing that the one I want is happy atleast,

Thats love,
And I know it does this to you and me.

Revolting Reality...

As I Stared into a dark form in the glass,
A voice inside asked me to go away somewhere far,
Away from who was looking back into my scars,
The eyes that looked were slowly eating,
The life left in my heart now emptying,
I remembered the years of my past,
And tears like rain kept falling fast,
My heart, its race, slowed down with time,
Only the pain of my form stopped me from dying...

'Hell Is Nothing Less Than The Absence Of The Beloved...'

Oh come on, its been so long,
Dont know what youre doing to me,
Youre going nowhere,
Youre coming no near,
Stuck everywhere where my eyes see,
Youre like a dream thats always and never mine,
Everyone and everything has a reflection of you,
I am so used to of missing you,
But what do i do to stop loving and needing you,
The flame of love flickers in my soul,
Making me hate and love you,
Oh come on, its been so long,
This pain that im used to, is still no good to me,
I cant make you love me,
Forgotten about all that crap,
But even now, youre still there,
Youre everywhere,
My heart has grown sick, it has shoved u away,
But my heart at the same time still wants you,
Youre stuck in me,
Youre stuck in me,
A part of my soul u were,
Every part in me was yours,

But youve gone,
Tears have flown,
The pain has made me insane,
Youve gone,
Taken with you an integral part of me,
Oh come on, i dont know what im doing,
Cant you see,
I need you like crazy,
Can you please get in front of me,
Oh, i know ure gone,
You are not coming here,
Why am I asking u to come to me,
We're no longer friends, just nothing at all,
I'm scared someone will replace you,
Baby, I love you,
Let this love live,
I dont want it to subside,
Please, this love is everything to me,
Cant give your space to anyone,
No, loving again is too much for me,
I'm sorry baby, I can't give up,
Ive come this far I can't give up,
Baby, do something,
I'm in hell till you come to me.

Elegy upon undoing love

There are too many words
To chose from amidst this gloom
Like tender sharp shards
Delightful sight, a lonesome doom

Such is love they say
Like the death of a dream
Upon some lovely stream
That holds a secret 'pay'

Sometimes the echoes from the past dim
As I move away from the shoreline
Yet in moments of solitude
My mind lets go
But the heart loves on
Ever imagining a lawn
Although it's gone
Washed with time and deceit
Dressed in memories that repeat

But I heave a heavy sigh
In the cold of reality
It's over now, so high
Her cruel duality!

I board another train, waiting enough
I saw her leave with someone else already
I realize she did not leave me very much,
Not even laughter. Not even laughter....

Oh woe! Why do I still love? Am I not killing myself thus?
I realize some chains can never be untied.
I remember she told me when she came, she was a stranger.
Yet I loved her.

Served love to lust - Vittal Acharya Vandavasu

"Hello sir, there's only 'bright darkness' on the menu"
"Oh well, can I smoke in here", said I to the waiter
He was waiting to see if I'd sell you
Yes you, dear reader. You.

You see I visited this bistro
A little time ago
With a woman I loved.
I presume I need not explain anymore.

So here we are with a bottle of rum
Drinking in such splendid honesty
She's with another, I am glum
But I never wanted to deceive you

I understand you might wonder
"Wait, how am I here?"
But you see you are still reading
For I have honestly conducted-

By chore of serving love to lust
And not presenting mundane poesy
But something interesting, anti-rust

Desperate rhymes yet honest words

Flamboyant times with vacant- "Waiter, I think I need another bottle",.

Dust and dreams - Vittal Acharya Vandavasu

I stood there looking,
but then I realized I wasn't.
I was just standing.
Now I can really look.

I wonder every night - Vittal Acharya Vandavasu

I wonder every night
When the night gets cold and lonely
And you are not in sight
I miss you and so dearly

A fear comes within me
A dark sadistic one
Are you mine to see?
Do we together run?

Another man would touch you
And plant his strange familiar kisses
In the places I did, a few
Oh! How this lover badly misses

Is he gentle to you?
Do you whisper his name into his ear
Like you did mine?
Do you feel lost in ecstasy
Remember we were lost in our arms….
I guess you know each other
Before, we laid eyes on us
So he never was a stranger

And I was never familiar

I was never the loved
I was part of a list
My sighs gently bowed
To some gloomy mist

Slytherin can I come in - Vittal Acharya Vandavasu

The brain's a gloomy thing
Seeks company of melancholy
Cunning, the song to sing
Adherence to wit's anatomy

To cast the darkest spell
Pure blood till the end
Where else to dwell
But at Slytherin's bend

A hint of pitch darkness
A means to all ends
Not evil in this paleness
But not ready for amends

While She Smiles Away - Vittal Acharya Vandavasu

Dreams turned to dust,
Sighs turned so cold,
My mind begins to rust
And love remains untold

Her hair danced with the wind
Mine was not allowed to
I wondered where was it I grinned
But somehow luck it flew

Then again I was always unfortunate
Ugly and lanky, eyes' discontent
And stares of disgust so importunate
But within lies some tender content

There lies a heart
No where to start
But things to part
Seem hard to dart

And so I still smile, while she smiles her smile away

She Stood There Alone - Vittal Acharya Vandavasu

The lights went out slowly
When all the people scurried,
One last gulp so lonely,
Gently, the wine hurried.

She smoked her cigarette to dreams
And drank herself to dream reality
When all the pills blur what seems
She knows lonely love is a fatality

She summoned her secret friend
someone she can talk to
There goes the smile, no amend
She got something to do

Then she realizes she's all alone
But she smiles, she doesn't sigh
She's only somewhere to be blown
She stood there alone, asking why?

I did not stay back - Vittal Acharya Vandavasu

I was looking at the star
It gave me an idea
like thoughts from afar
I found my dear

I decided to commit suicide
I can't say I was planning
But I was tired of homicide
I do it everyday, smiling

Plasticine smiles and fake handshakes
"I love you", oh what an abuse!
Life is touched by sullen brakes
And all of this is a gentle muse

That star still stayed on
I should have stayed in my room
Muttering and letting a moan
I should have let it gloom

But I came out
And climbed the stairs

Oh! what clout
I plunged into stares

I heard something wail - Vittal Acharya Vandavasu

It rained like the heavens were crying
I had no tears to hide so I shot an umbrella
I felt a little nervous through all this scurrying
And the rain stopped like a tired memorabilia

The trees whispered in darkness
While the night listened
My lamp was drenched in meekness
something unknown glistened

I heard someone running, my heart raced
I turned back but you'd know there's nothing.
I walked on with a little stiffness, amazed;
Fear started whispering tales, I wasn't fainting.

Something started wailing somewhere further
It was a woman's voice,"why did they do it?".
I walked to see her on the road in cold weather
She stood there with her face hidden every bit

She didn't notice me yet, I was afraid to move
Her hands hung limp on her sides unmoving
Her sobs and muttering had an eerie groove

I was entranced in fear and time was ruining

Her crying stopped abrupt, she started giggling
My lamp told me she looked at me through the hair
She started walking towards me, actually wiggling
"You'll do it too, come lets play',. I killed my stare-

-and ran back
I heard her cold laughter
My lamp was black
Her sound grew dim thereafter

I collided into something and fell
They pulled me up and stood
I saw her with a lamp, I'd yell-
-but nothing would hear, I understood.

Ode Upon Loneliness

There is this room
Which holds a window
I'd like to learn
To sweep my shadow

I do not like its company
It follows me all around
I crave a silent symphony
Not a clanging sound

My books and all my cigarettes
Drain my lovely wine
I hum a song I haven't met
By all the roads I dine

I don't know what I wait for
But I know that I am waiting
Nobody knocks anymore
Because they know I'm waiting

I miss that song

The barley danced and waved
While I strolled by
Solitude was gently paved
I heave a little sigh

I started to strum my guitar
I weaved a song around it
Alone and long and oh! so far
I smiled at my distant wit

She was so near I barely saw her
Because that was all I saw
I searched things far yes sir!
That's how I broke the law

I saw her finally when she walked away
The theme of everything I searched in vain,
I miss that song we used to sing yesterday
I miss that dance we never had in the rain

Those Tired Eyes - Vittal Acharya Vandavasu

Monday brought along with it-
-a strife to pardon glee
Without a place to sit
I'm sorry that I'm free

But still I hope to be
A little vacant rusty tool
That crafts a way to flee
Away from every tired fool

They talk and talk
But don't get paid
Yet still they talk
No dreams are laid

So many dreams
Have gone to dust
These endless streams
They talk to lust

And then a dreamers eyes
Get tired of all this fuss

And all those lonely sighs
Depart in the darkest bus

Some Distant Spring - Vittal Acharya Vandavasu

There used to be a girl
She liked to hold my hand
Oh! such a lovely pearl
I'd love to understand

We sang and ran
Through all the streets
She tossed a pan
I caught them sweets

She was my fan
And I was hers
Some masterplan
Some red flowers

But she began to bore
She got sick of it all
She stopped to adore
She stopped to call

She had other friends
she wasn't lonely like me
All her fancy trends

From afar I see

I wish she liked me too
I'd be smiling along with her
But, away she flew
Somewhere far away

Withered wings of little boys - Vittal Acharya Vandavasu

He saw the naked truth
But never realized it was naked,
They gave him a fruit
He never wanted to eat or fake it

They stamped it into him.
He thinks everything's clothed,
He'd like it only slim
and reserved what he loathed

He laughed in brittle silence
While they judged him for what he was
He talked in whispered eloquence
Everyone nodded and gave a pause

Dreams were made, they weren't dreamed,
Lies were told but weren't made.
Deaf when innocence screamed,
His smile began, to slowly fade.

He passed on the fruit
Entwined in the mad ritual
His boy would never loot

His father robbed perpetual

Where would he fly?
Where could he run
So he learned to sigh
And be no one

Ah! Look at these boys
Society's finest toys

When we part forever

My love I look at you like a prized possession
Would you still be there on the day?
When I can no longer look?
Or would you fade away like possessions do upon death?

www.ingramcontent.com/pod-product-compliance
Lightning Source LLC
LaVergne TN
LVHW050425160726
843469LV00041B/1231

* 9 7 8 9 3 5 6 1 0 4 8 1 5 *